SCANDINAVIAN FOLK DESIGNS COLORING BOOK

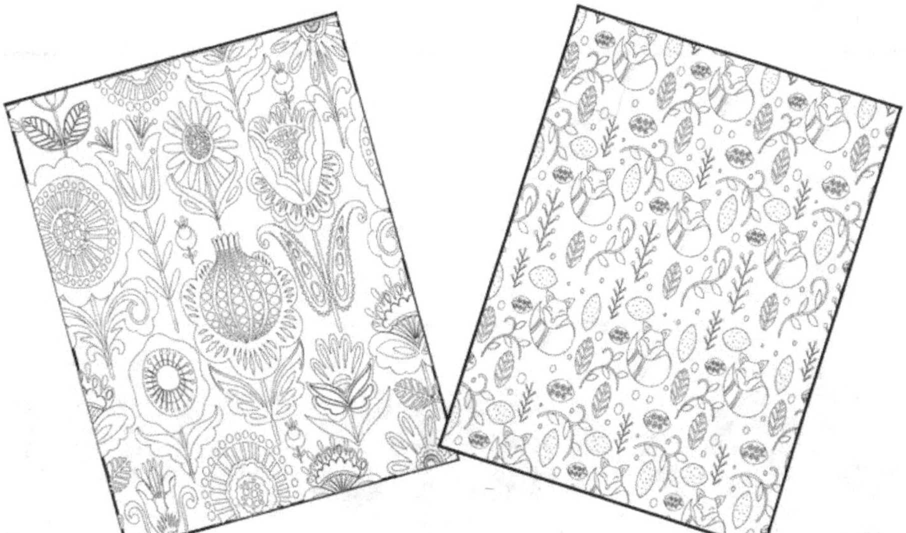

THIS BOOK BELONGS TO :

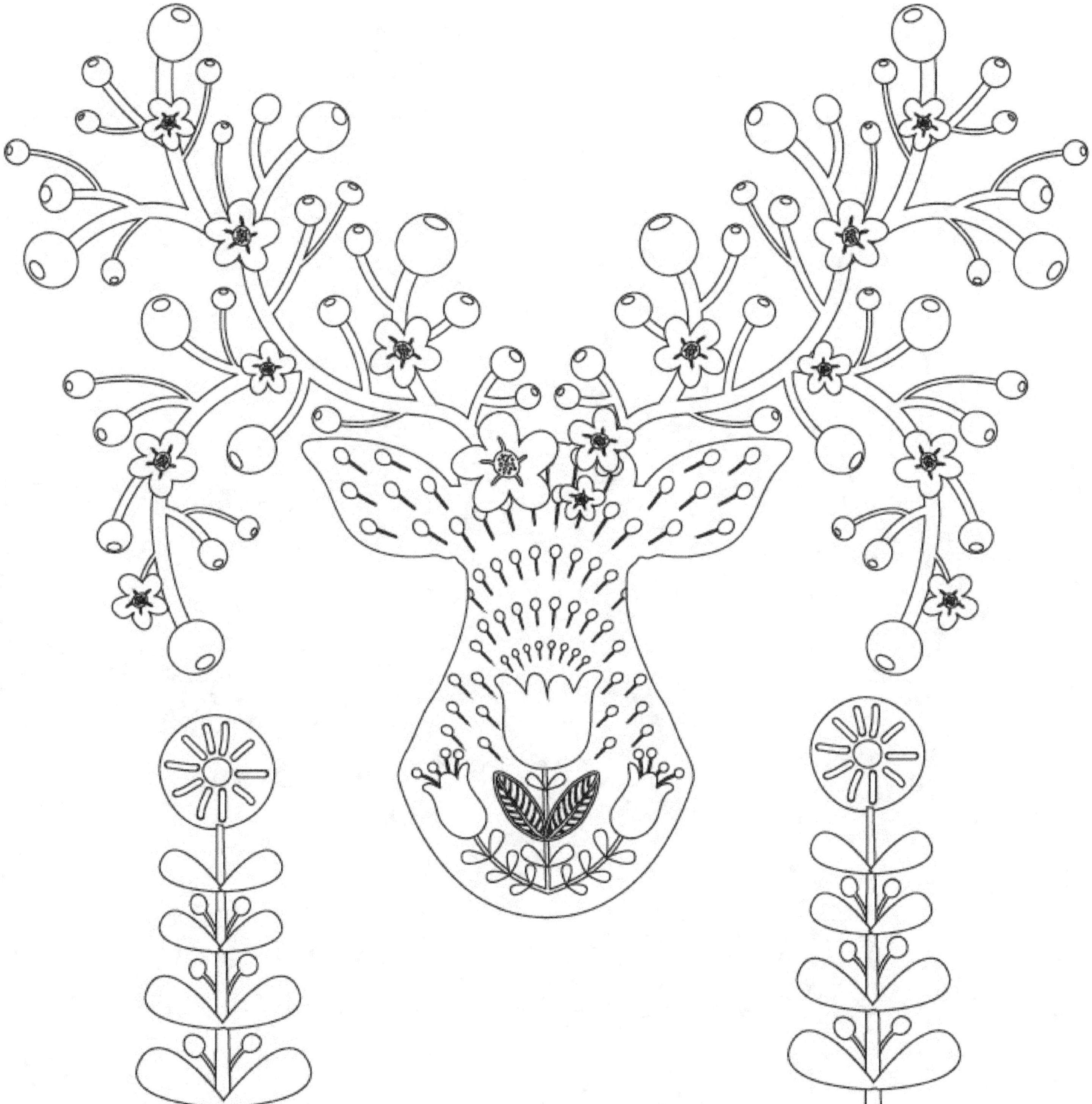

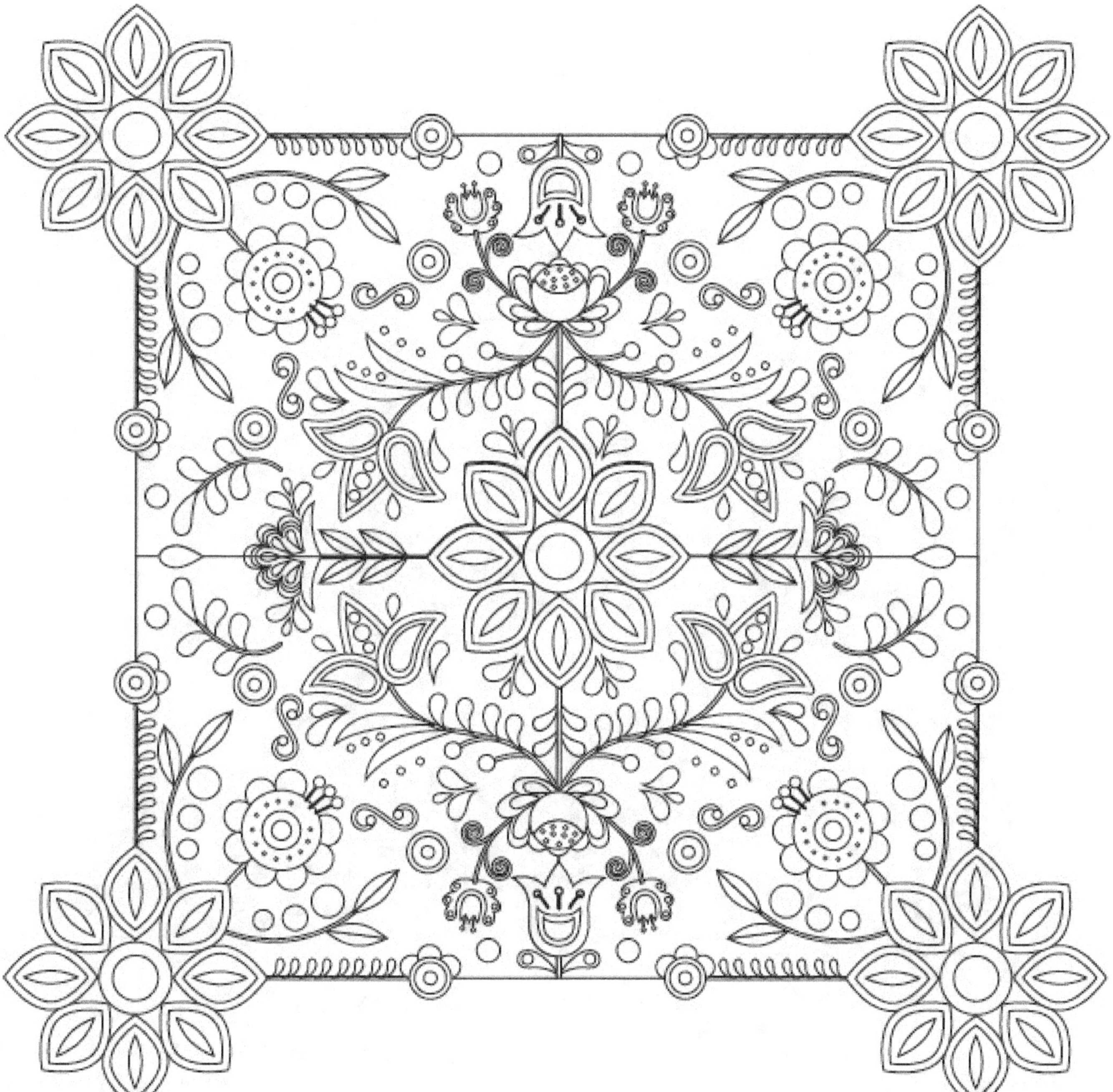

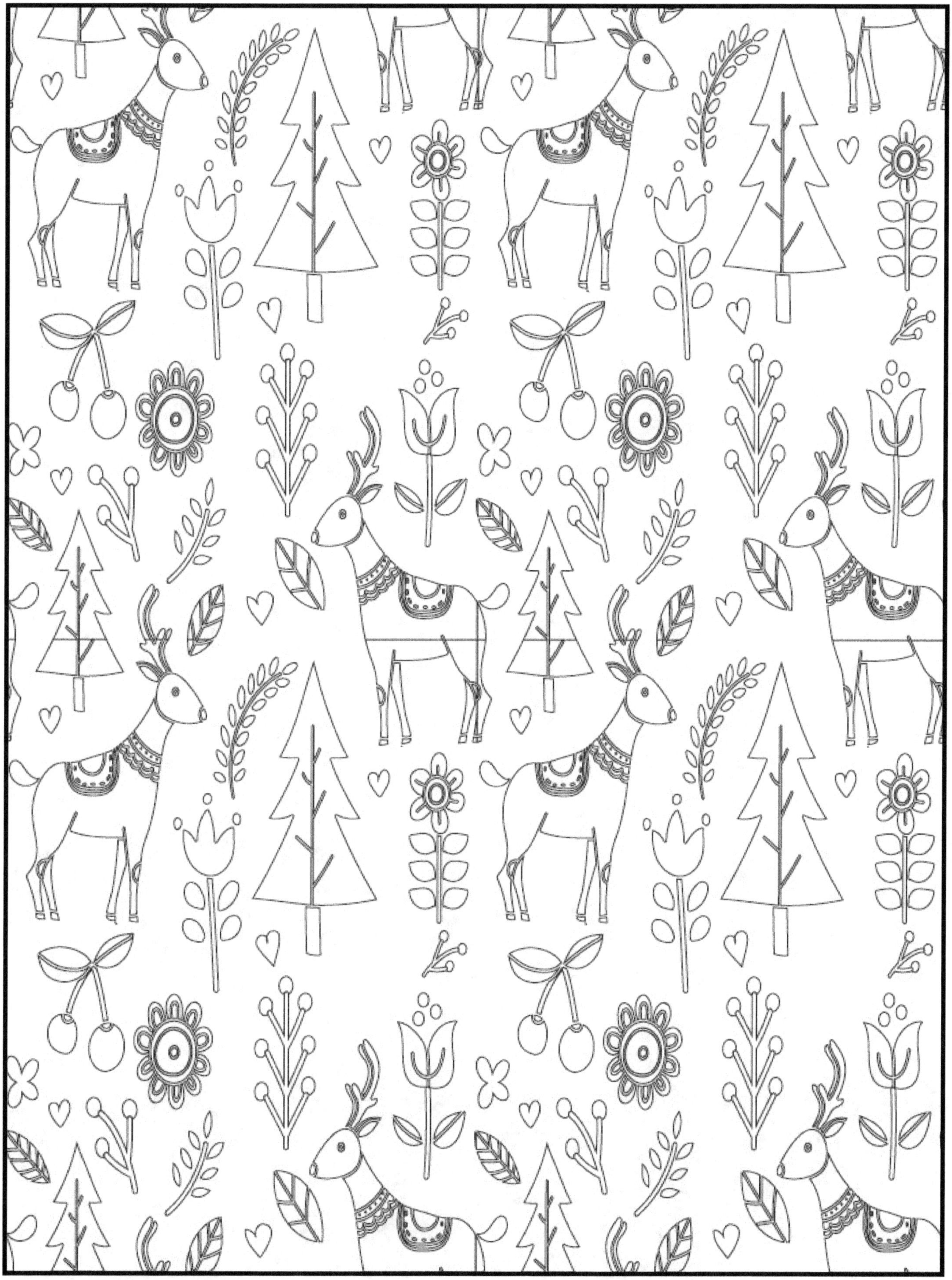

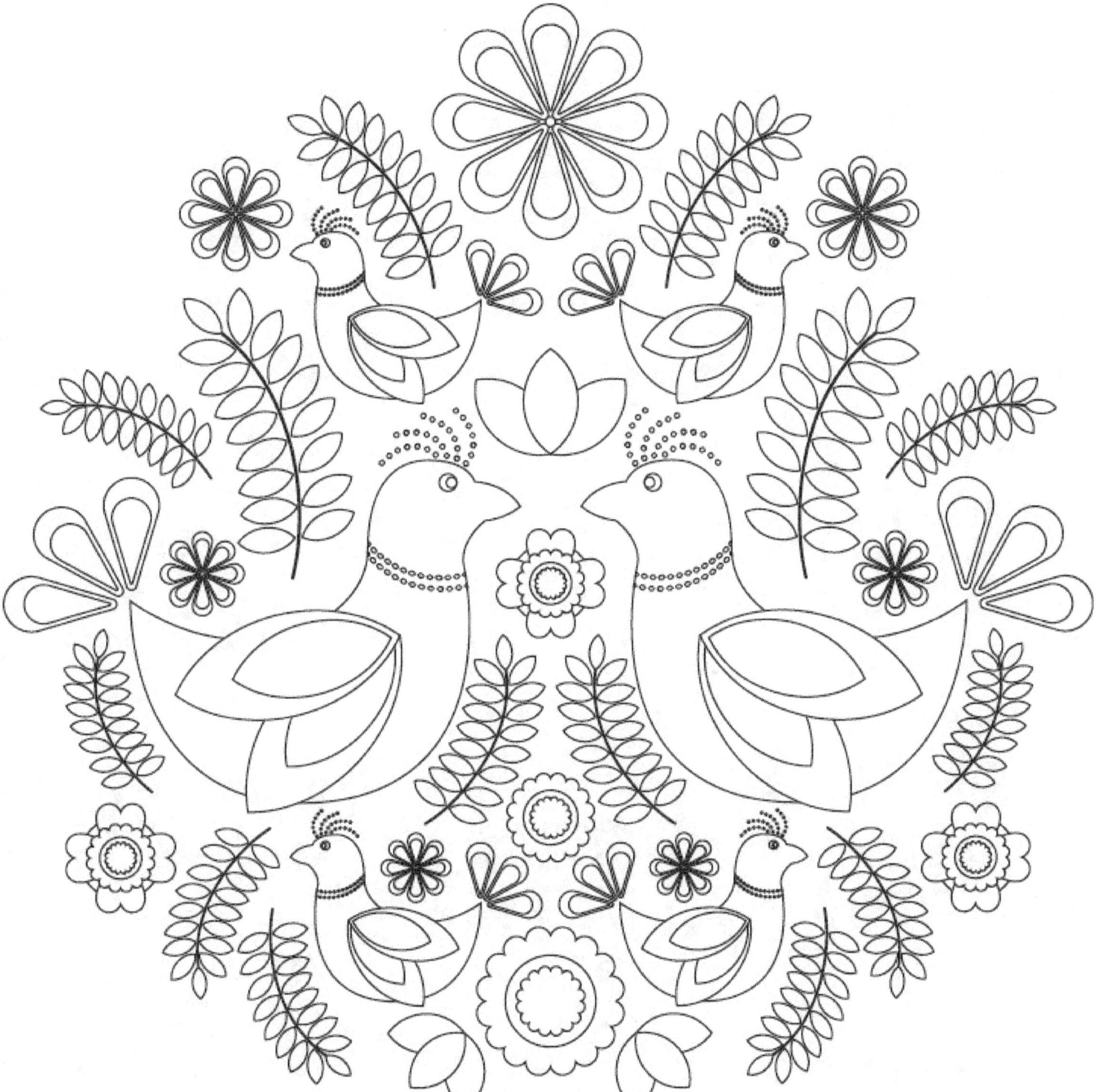

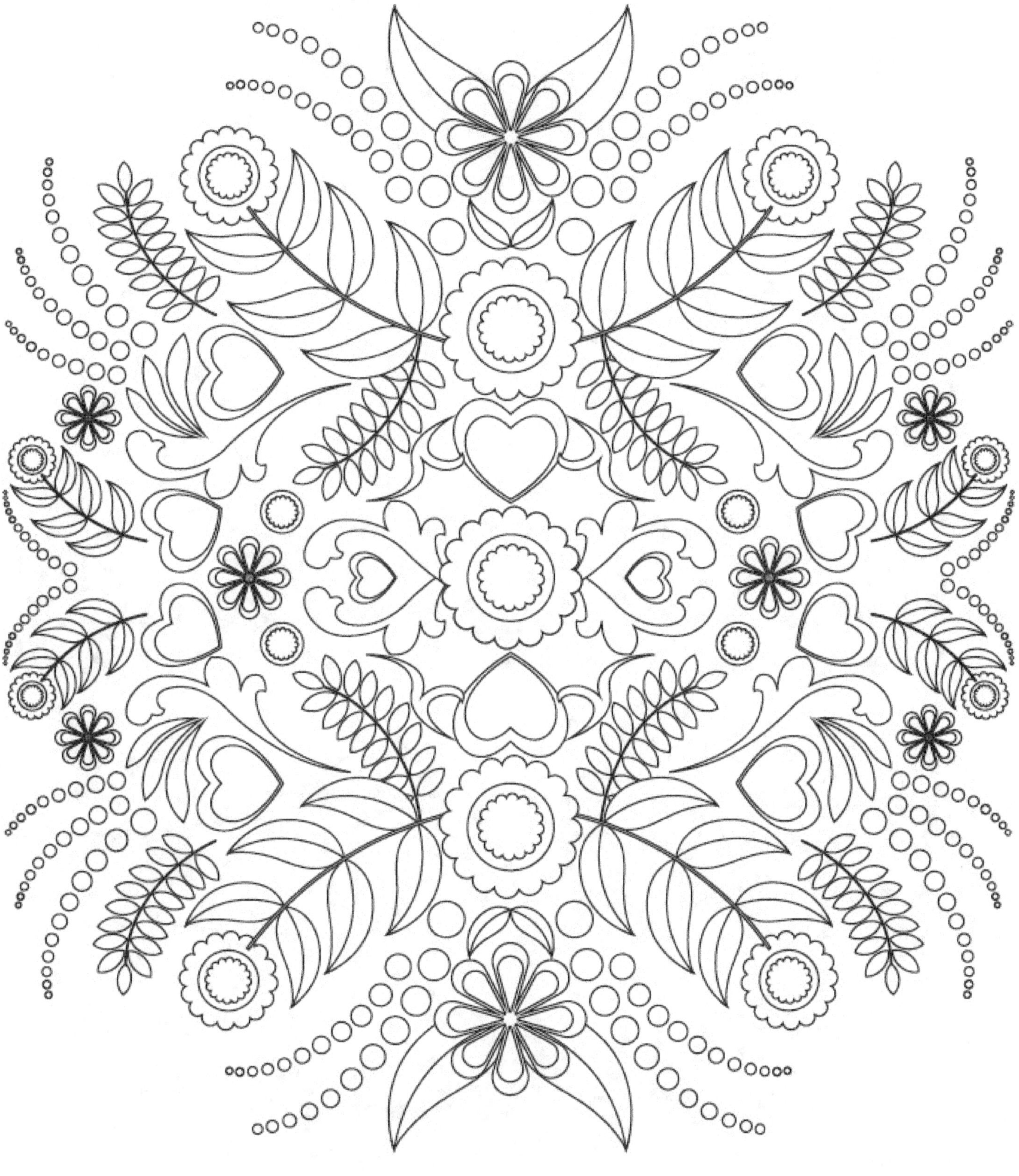

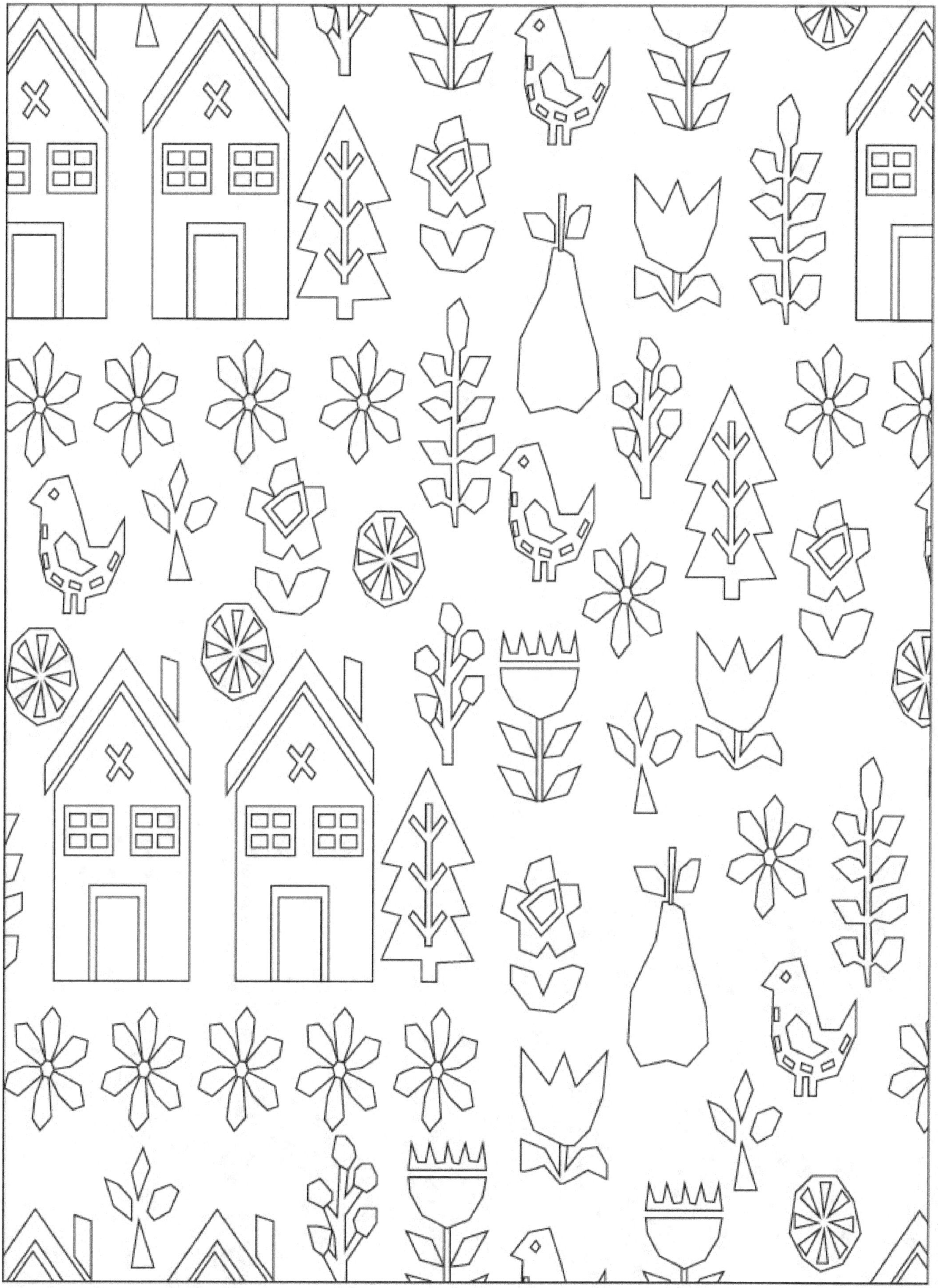

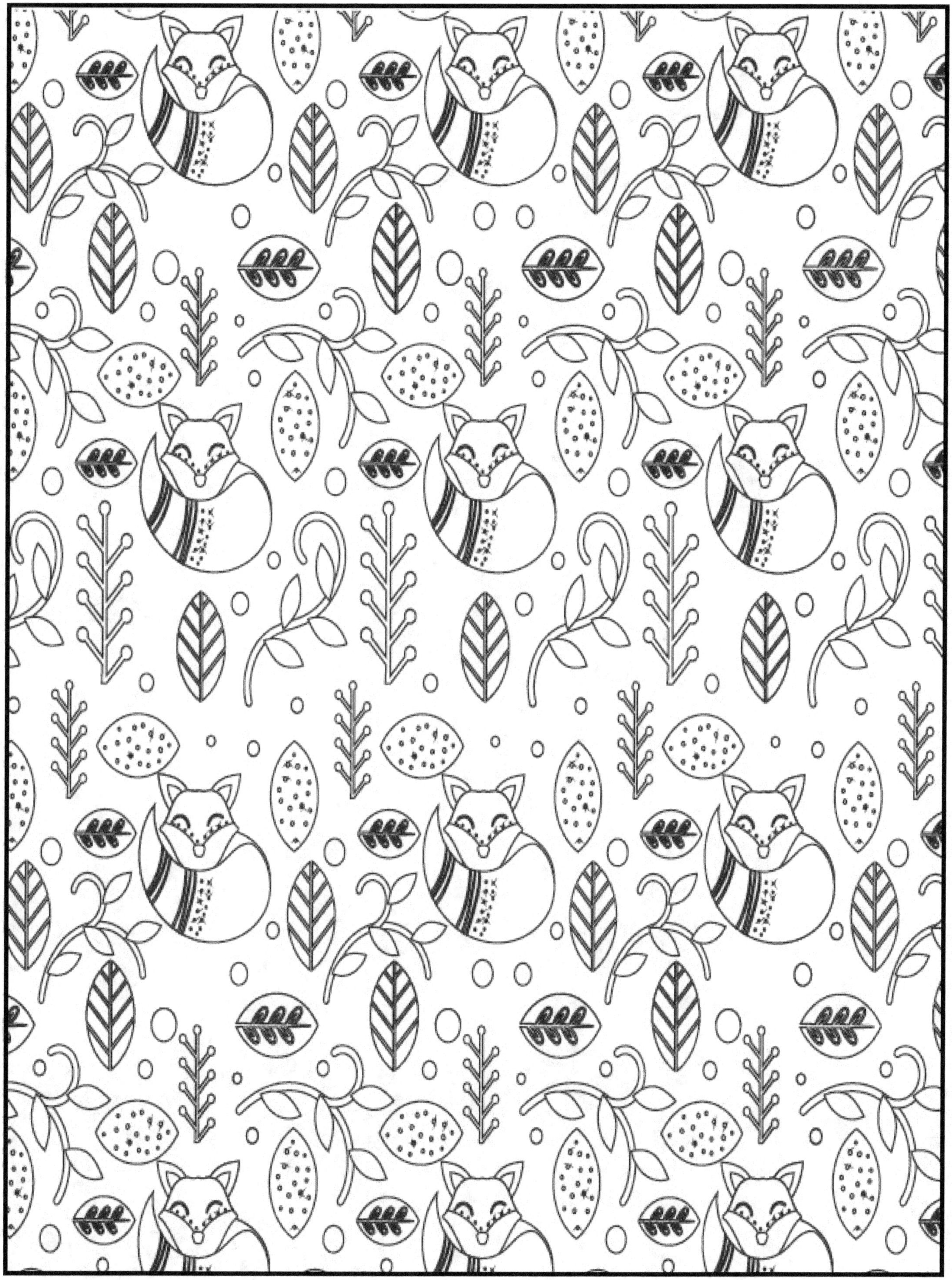

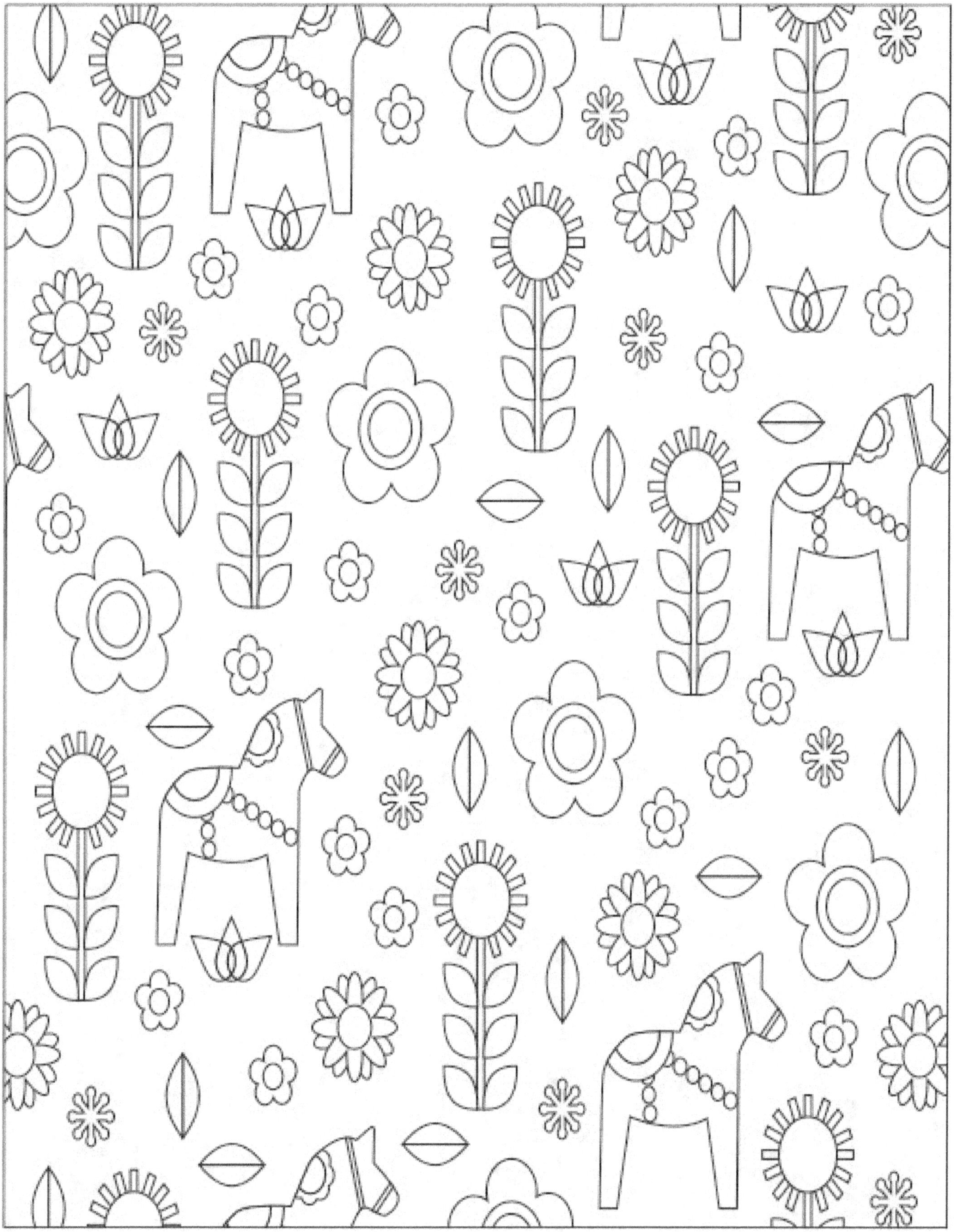

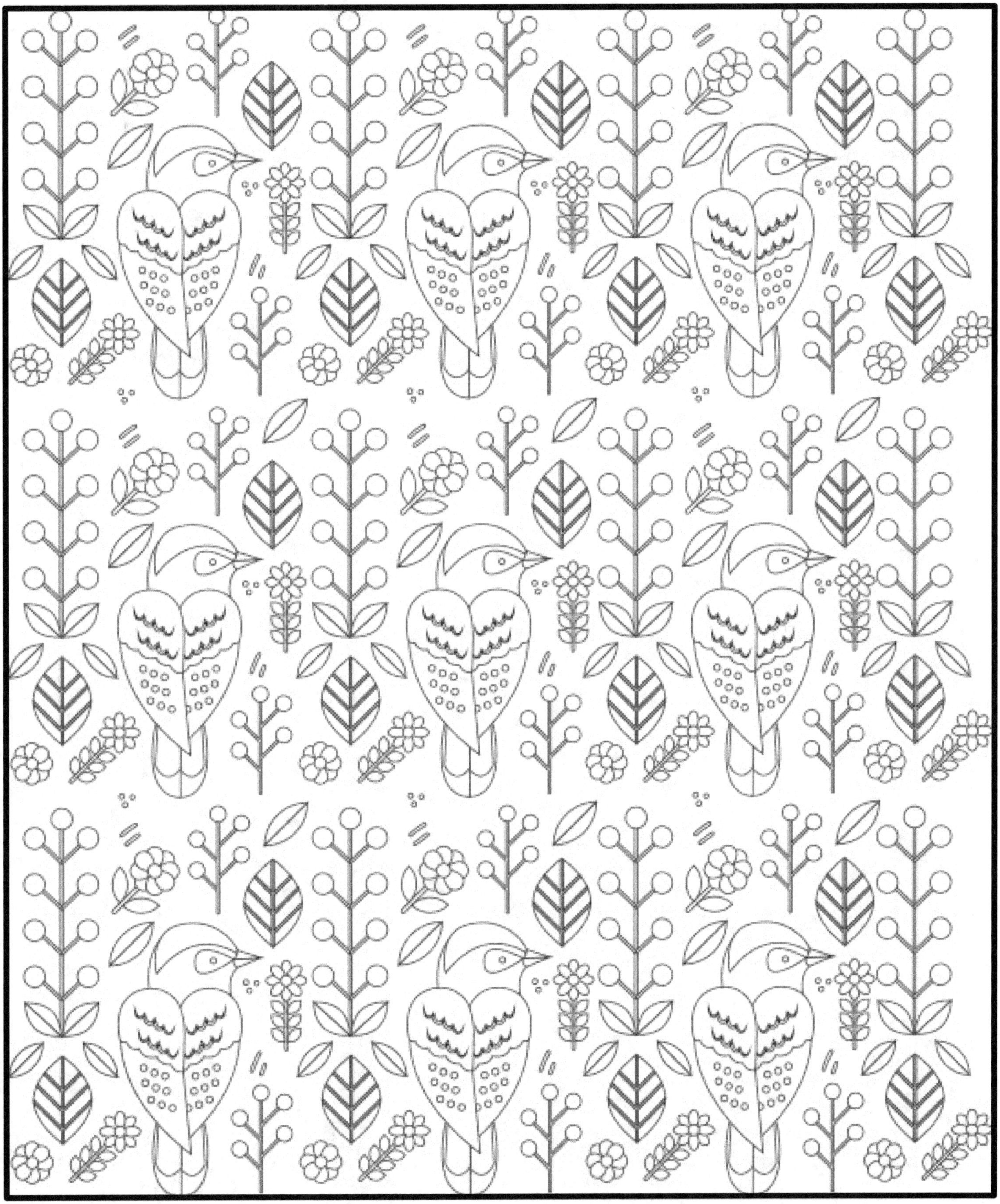

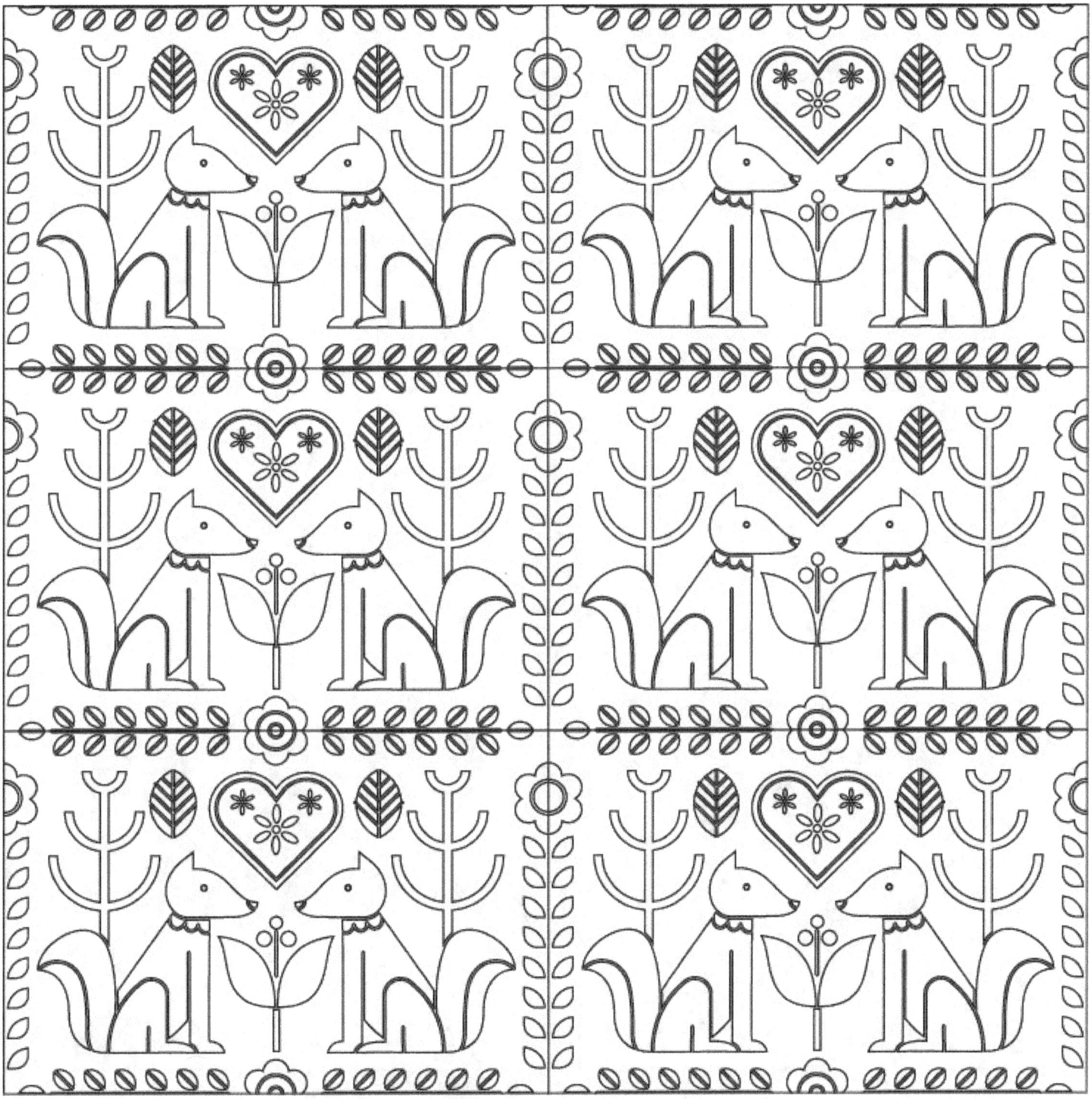

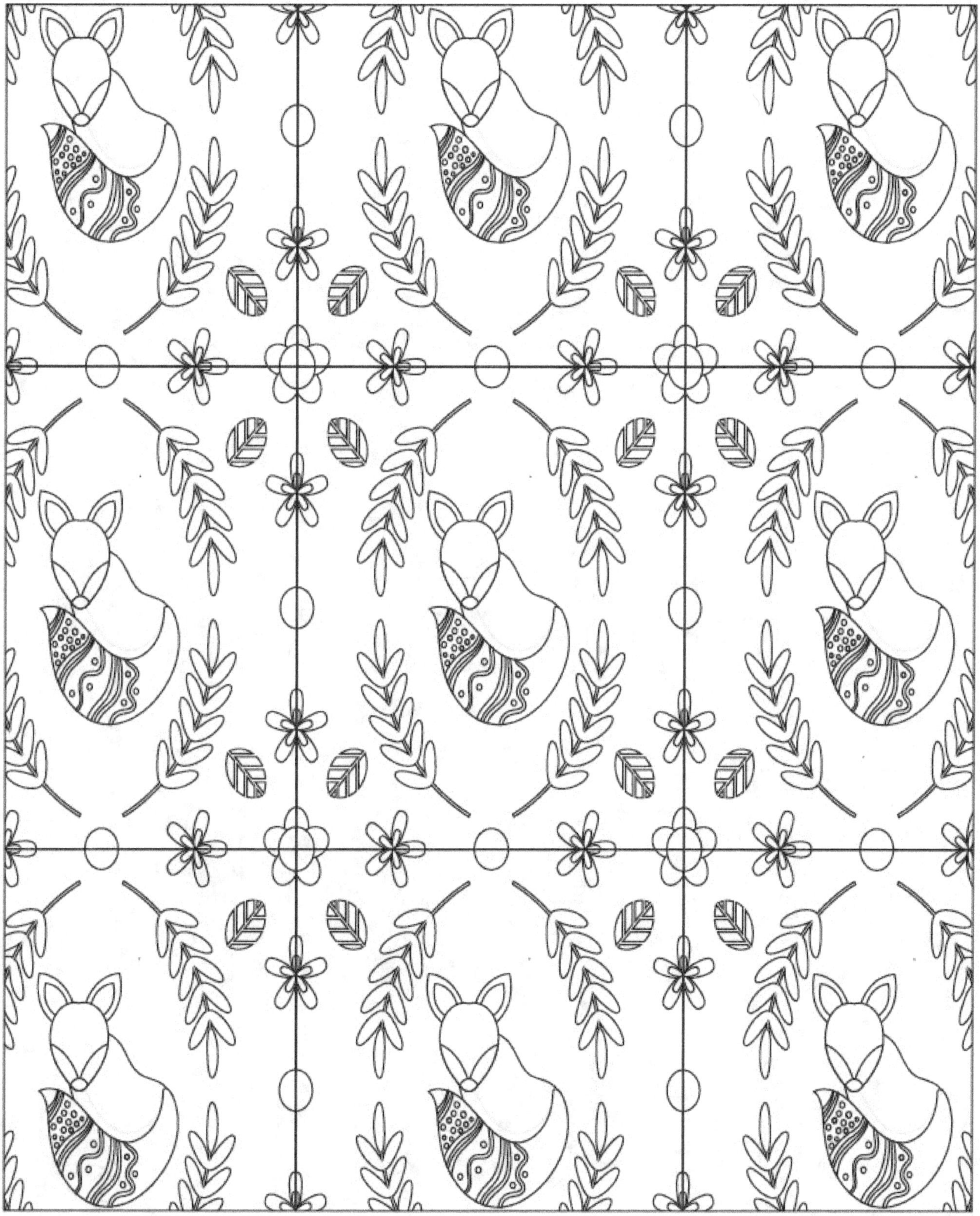

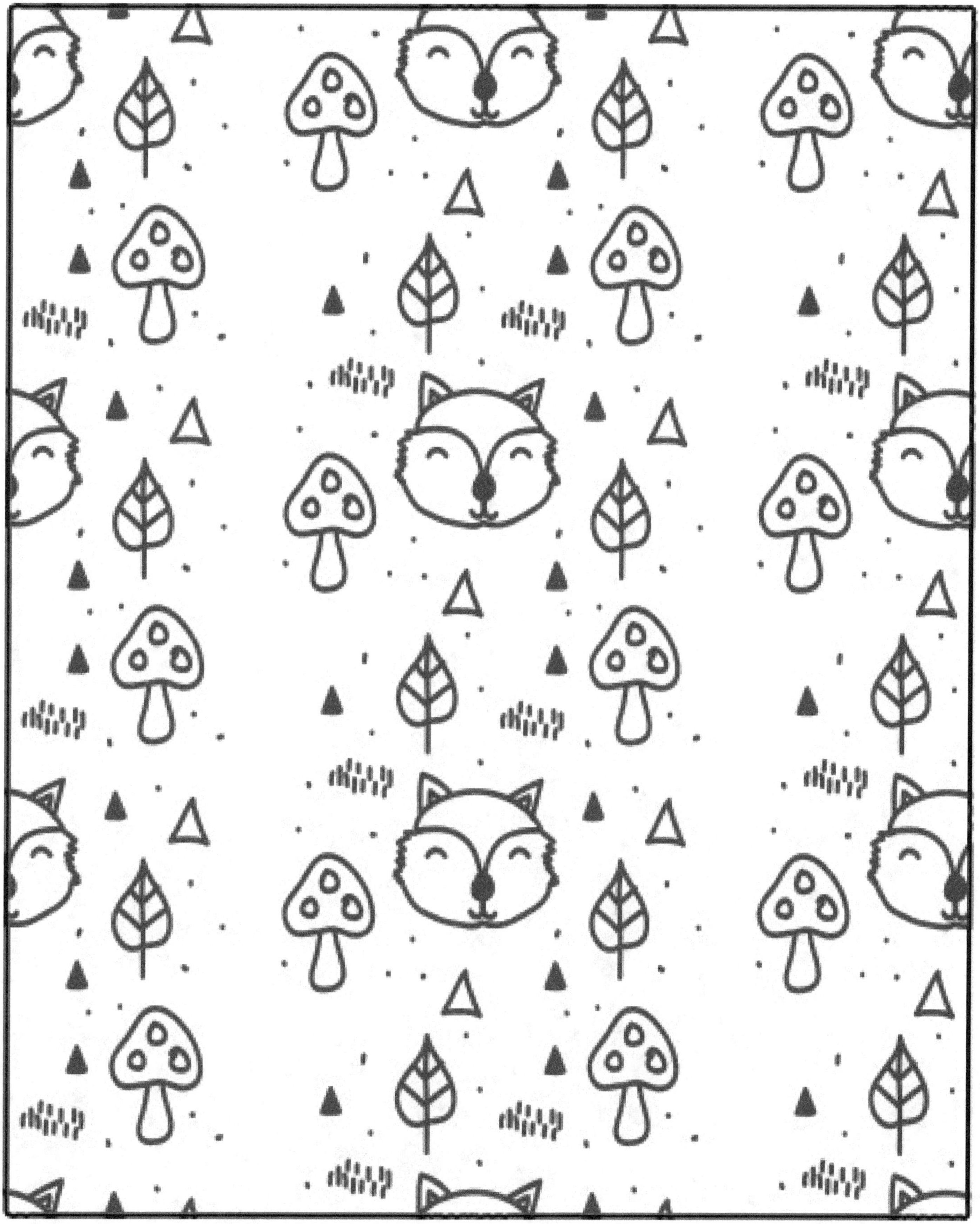

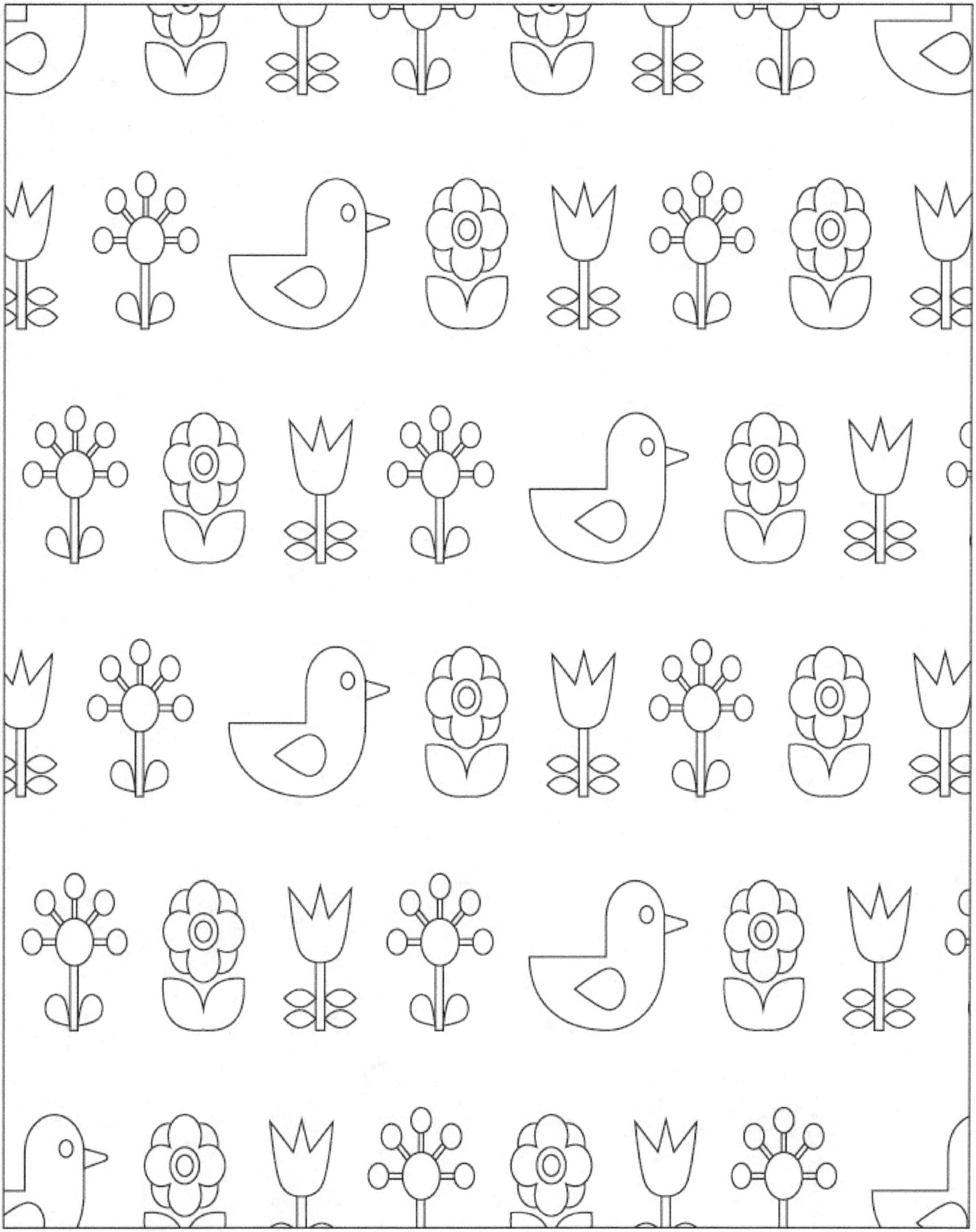

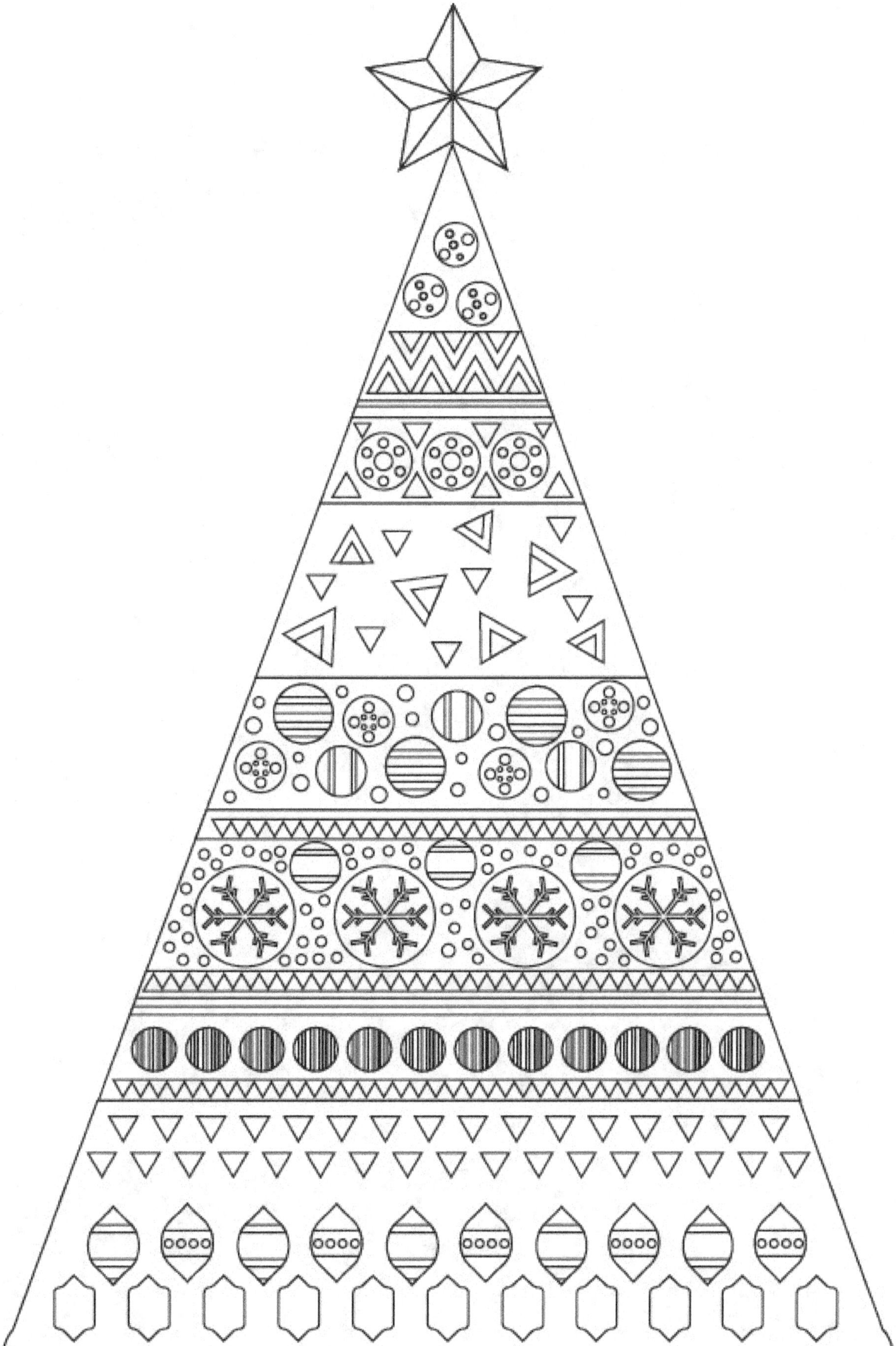

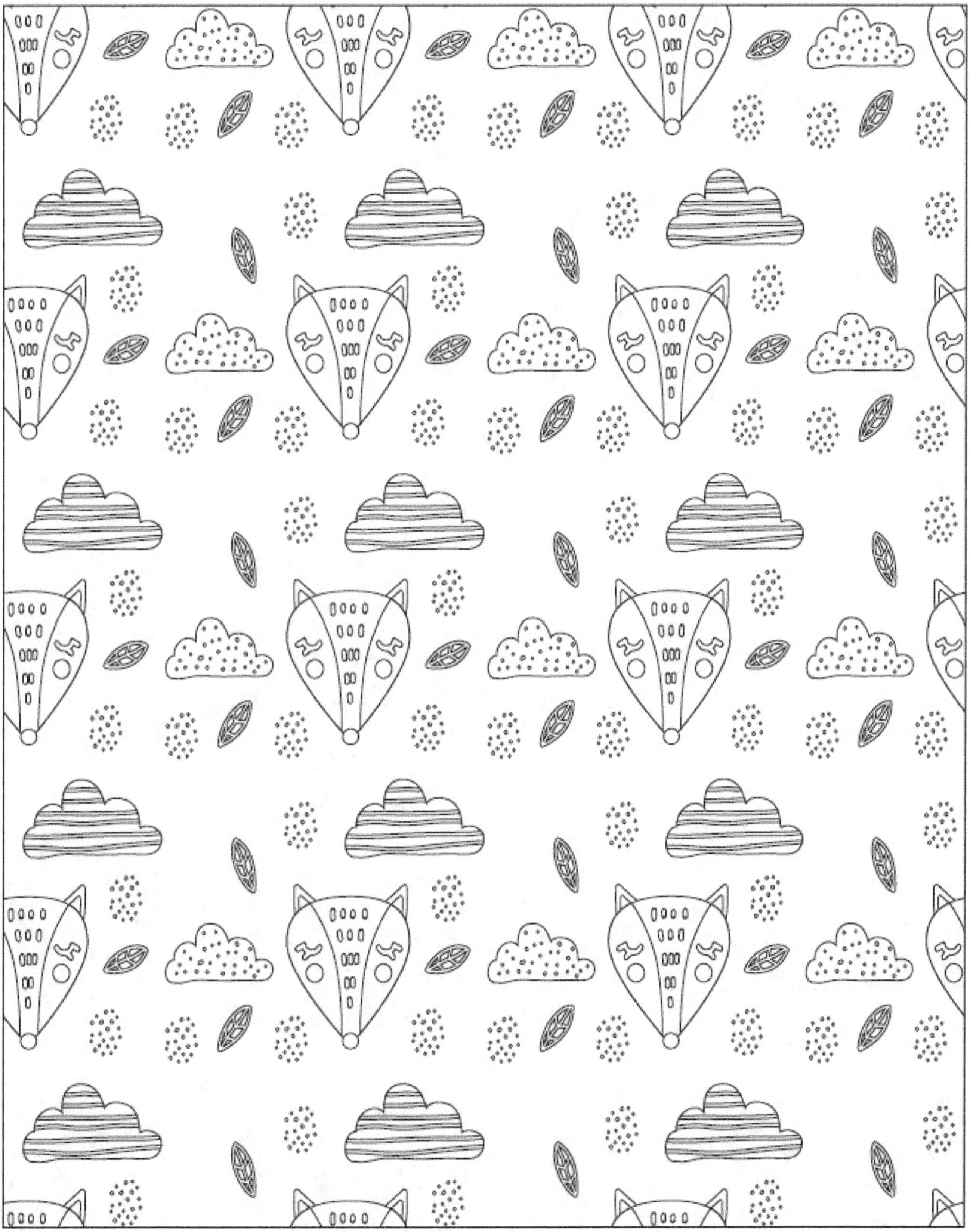

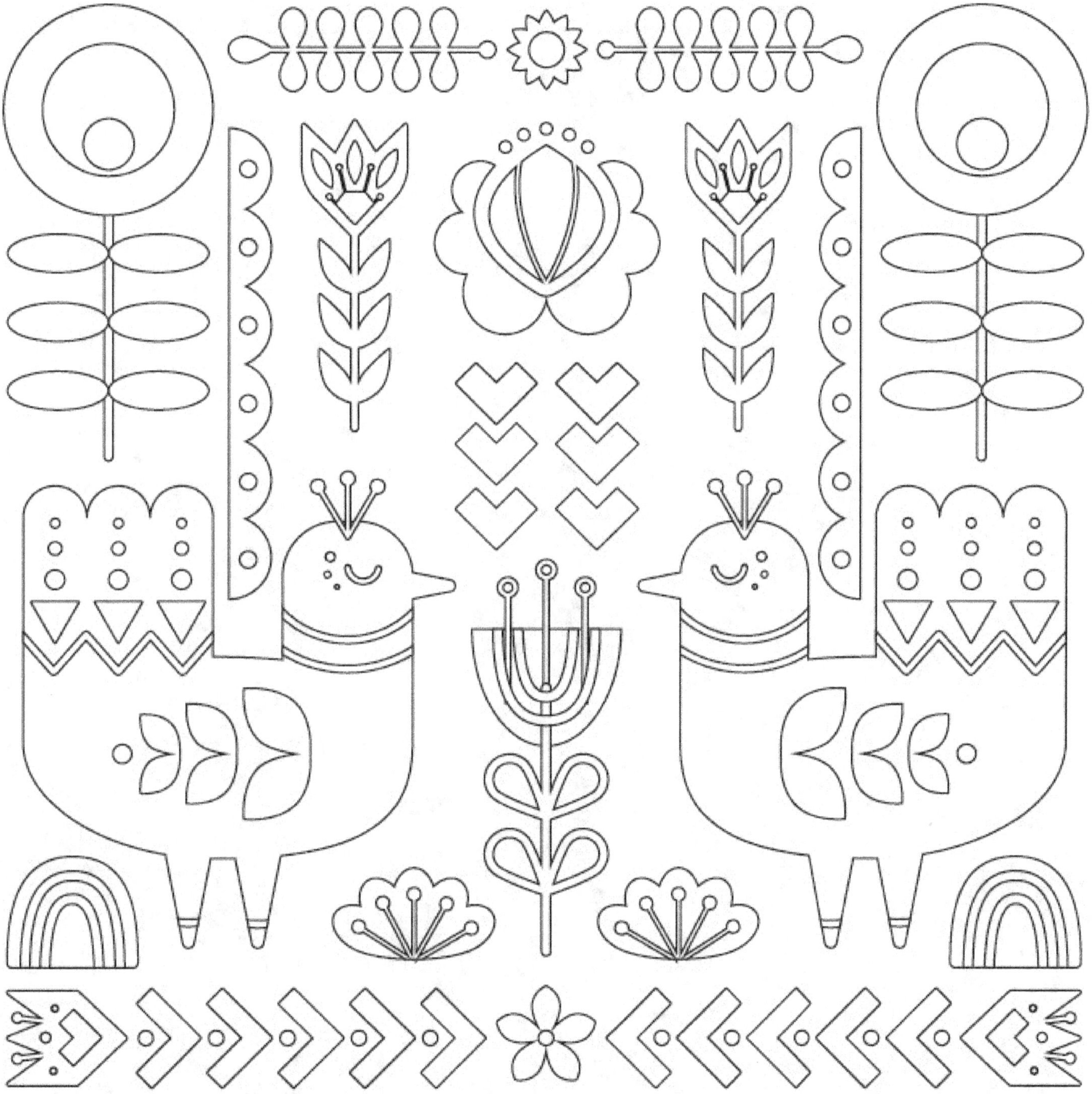

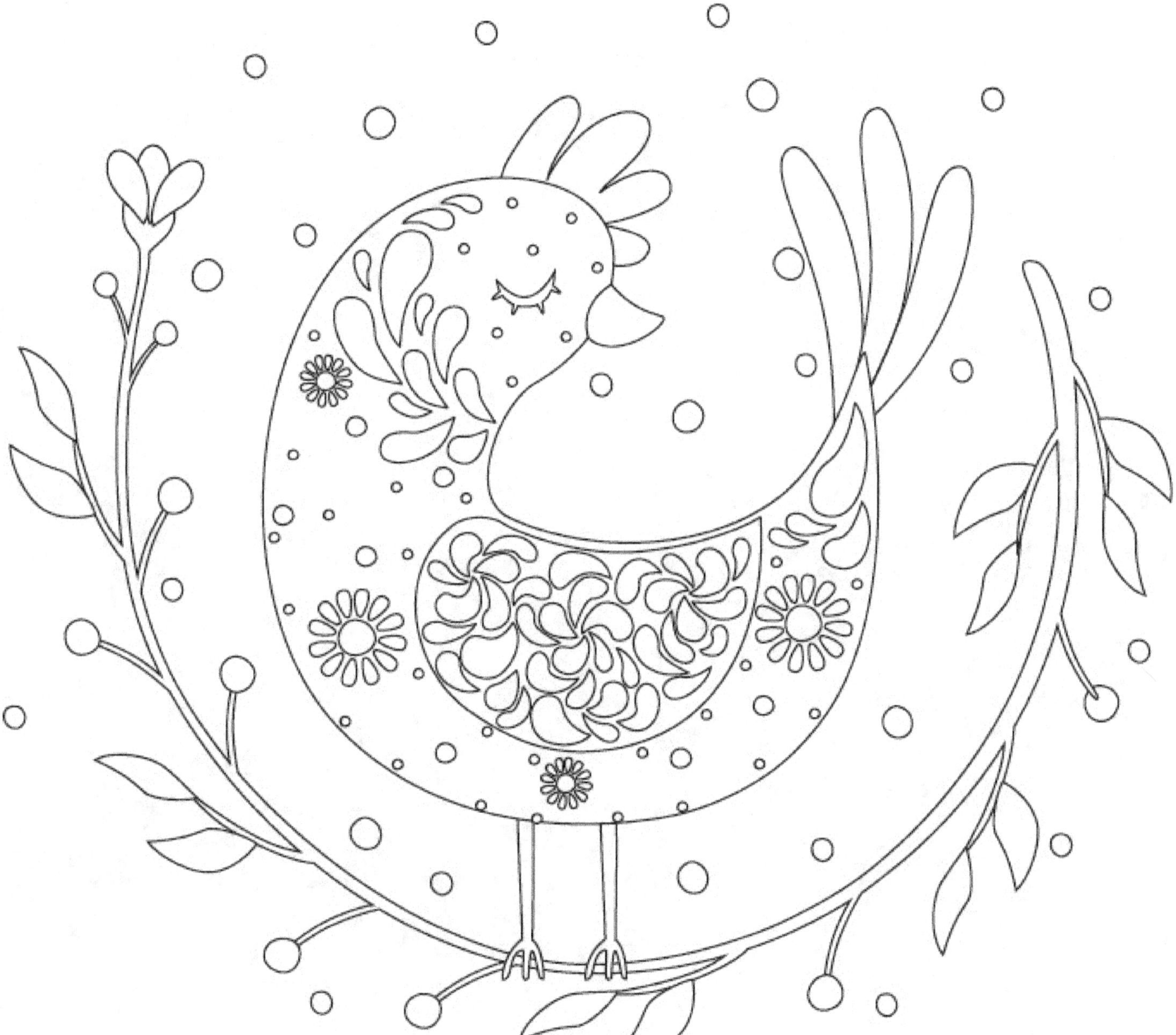

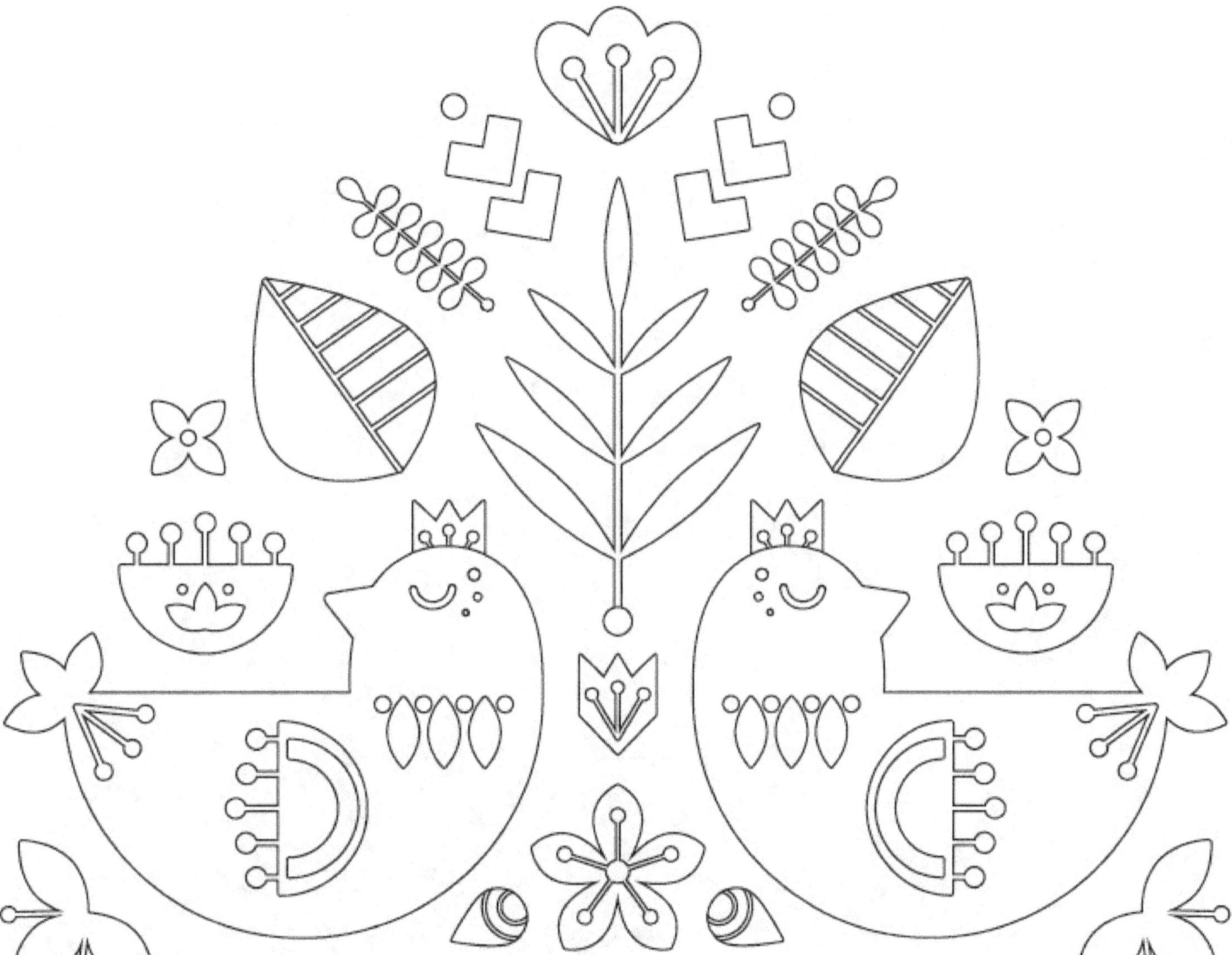

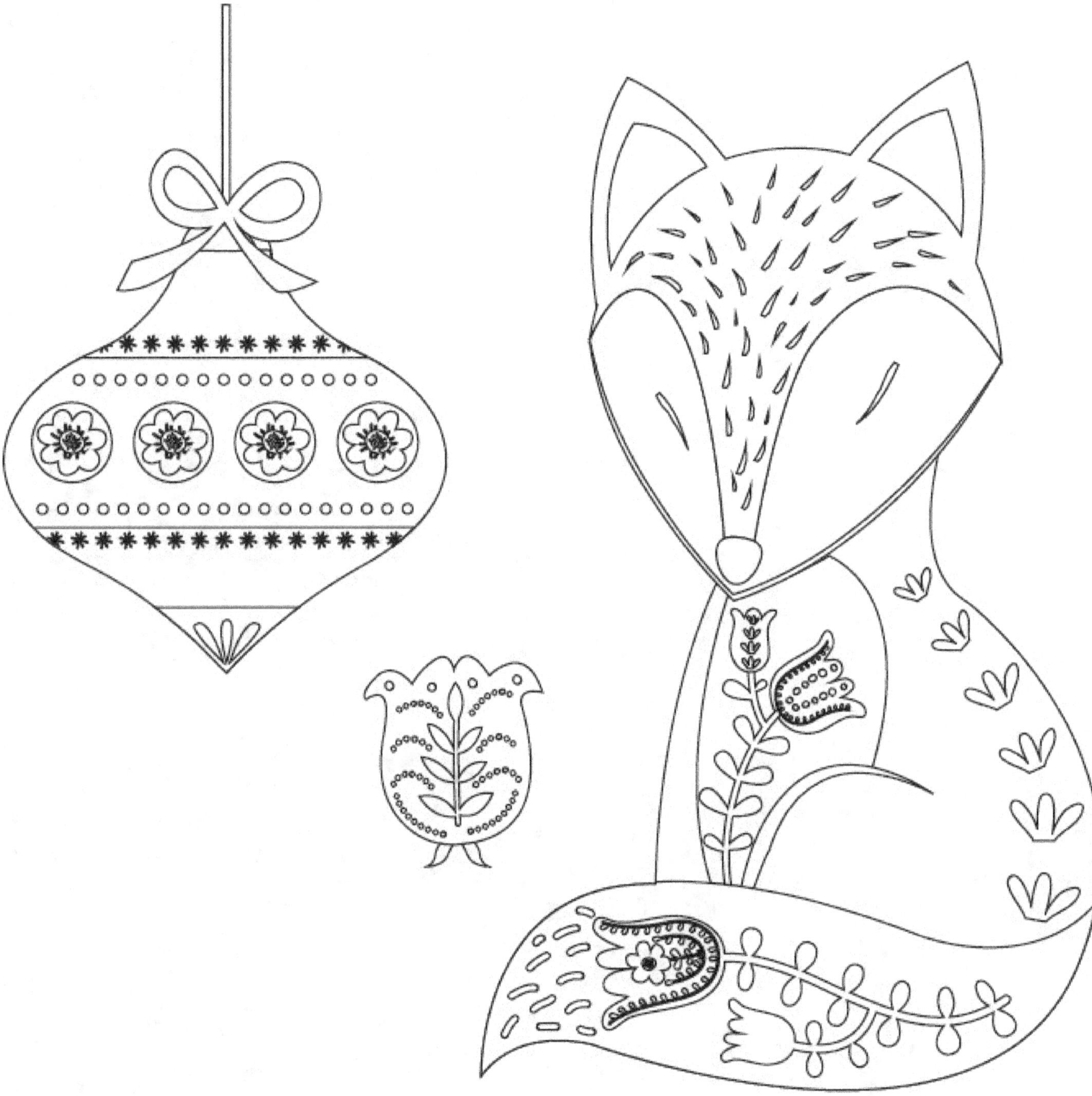

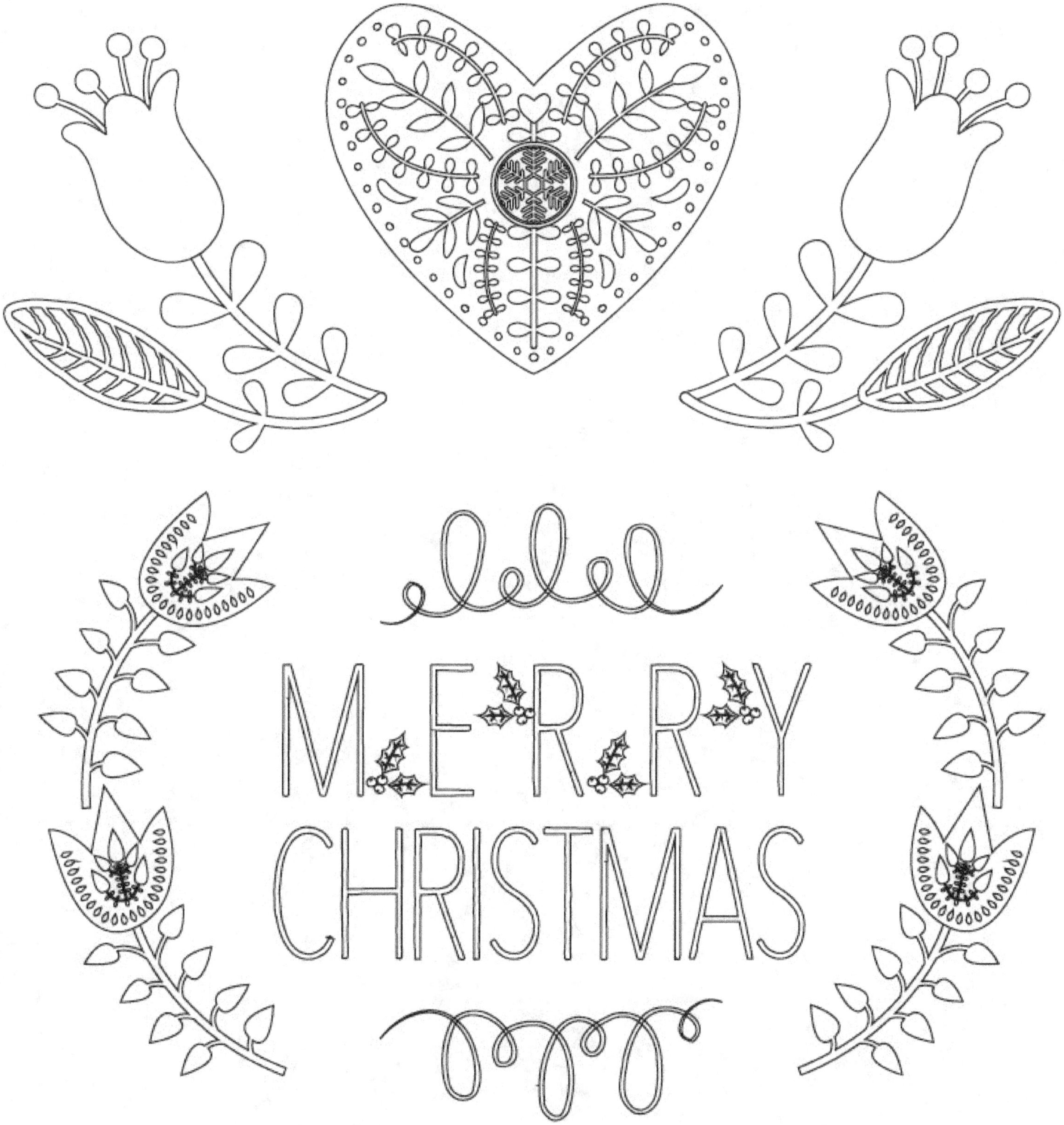
MERRY
CHRISTMAS

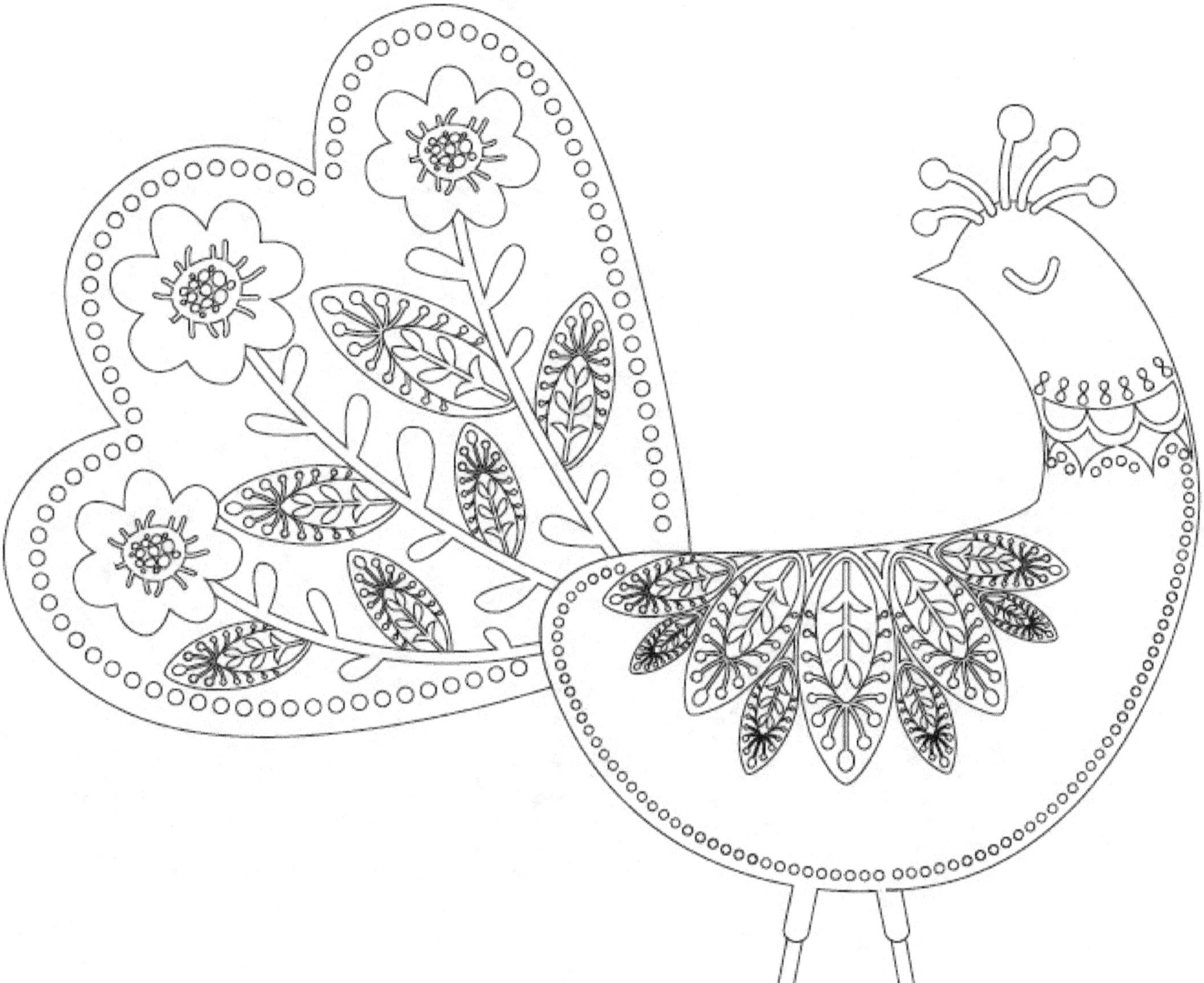

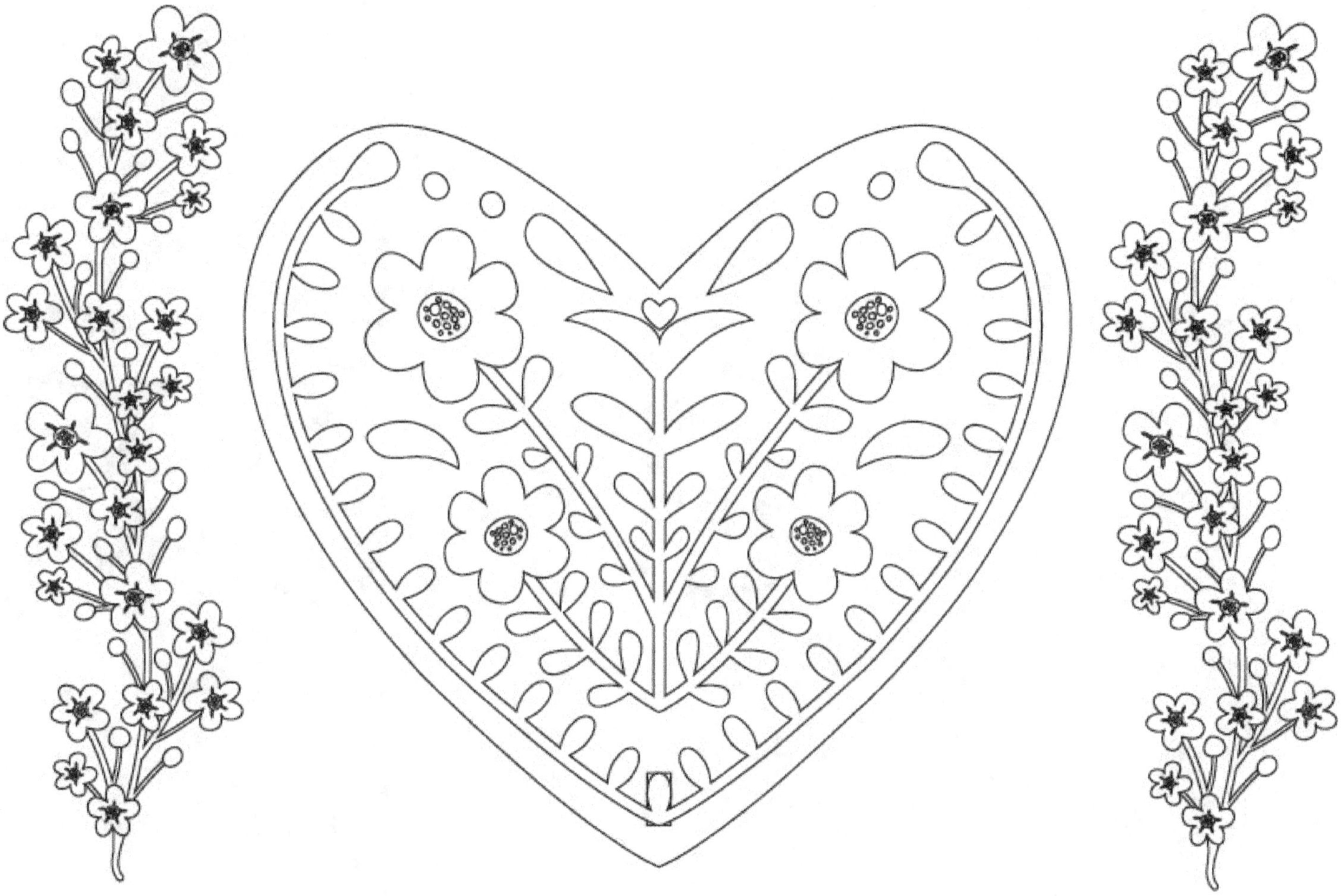

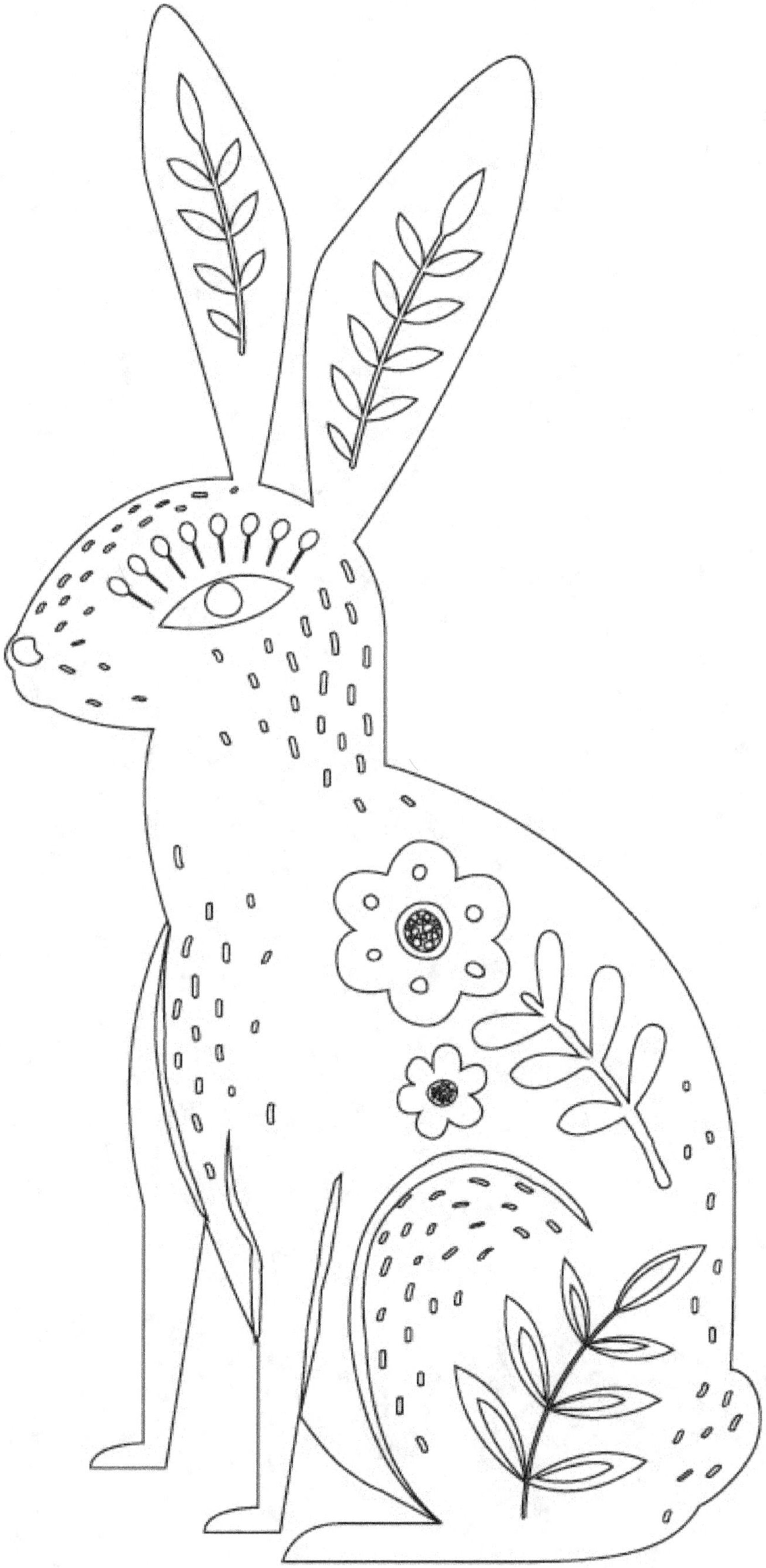

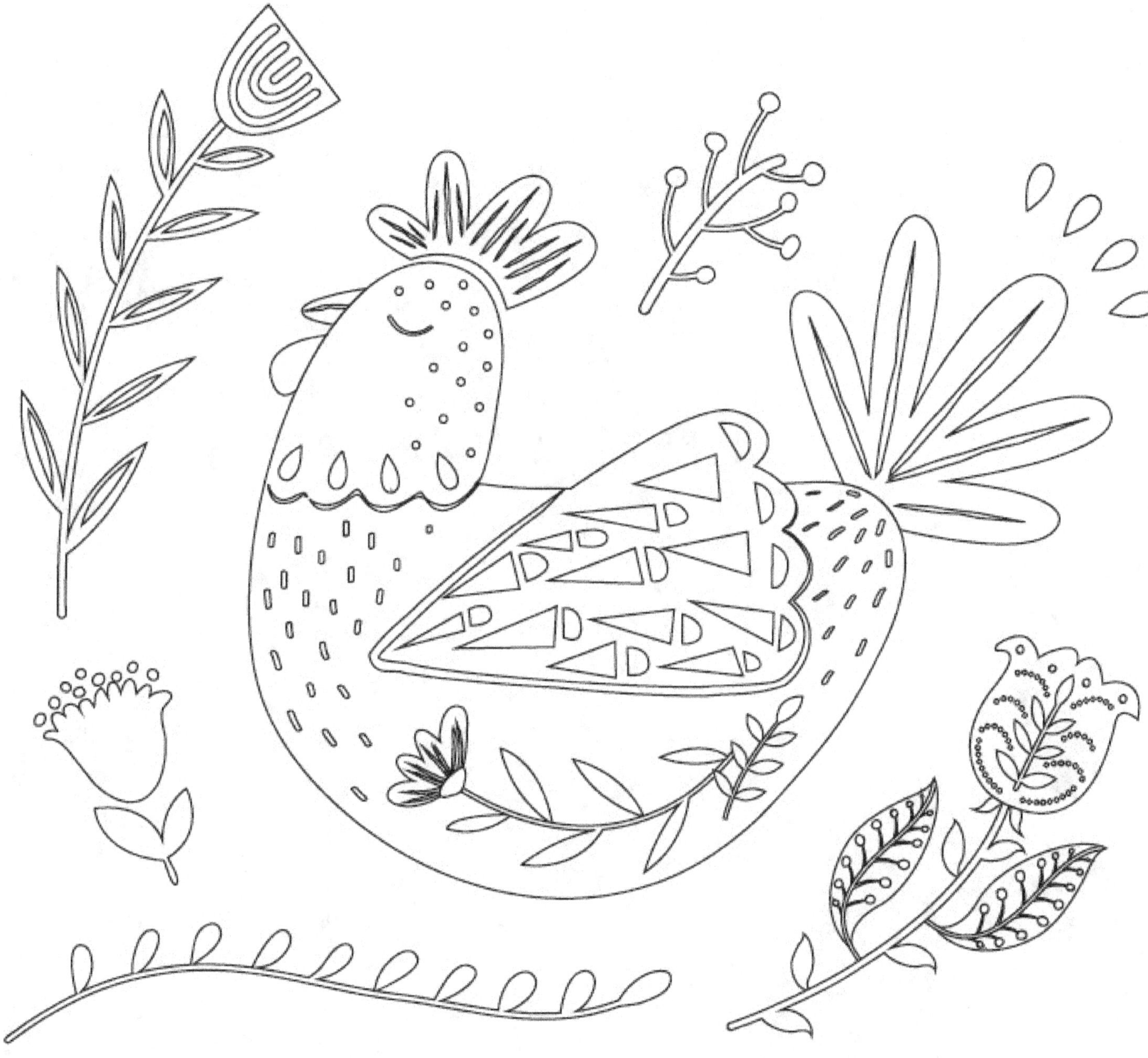

www.ingramcontent.com/pod-product-compliance
Lightning Source LLC
Chambersburg PA
CBHW081539220526
45467CB00010B/3257
9798695858792